GEORGIA'S GREAT UNDERTAKING

THE BEGINNINGS OF THE
WESTERN & ATLANTIC RAILROAD

GEORGIA'S
GREAT UNDERTAKING
THE BEGINNINGS OF THE
WESTERN & ATLANTIC RAILROAD

Linda Hewitt

Maps drawn
by
Robert Hewitt

ArbeitenZeit Media

ISBN 13 Kindle Edition: 978-1-941168-09-7
ISBN 13 Trade Paperback Edition: 978-1-941168-08-0

An Original Work
Georgia's Great Undertaking: The Beginnings of the Western & Atlantic Railroad is an original work by Linda Hewitt (14 04 05)

Maps

The future is born in dreams.

In the history of Georgia, as in that of all states, are several clear turning points characterized by a change in policy or activity that had significant impact on the state's subsequent development. Frequently these turning points have occurred in times of flux when traditional approaches have proven inadequate to meet some new challenge.

The new challenge in the United States of the 1820s and 1830s was a frantic commercial rivalry among the Atlantic seaboard states to capture the lucrative trade of the rapidly growing West. The favored instrument for securing this trade was the internal improvement — the road, the canal, the railroad. A spirited competition began that would decide which state would benefit most from the growth and westward spread of the nation's population.

Georgia's response to this challenge was to create in 1836 the Western and Atlantic Railroad (W&A). This line, which runs northwest from Atlanta, connects Georgia's other railroads with the transportation systems of states to the west. Modern historians have described it as the cornerstone upon which rests the transportation advantage that has made possible much of the economic development of the state. Some go so far as to give it credit for Atlanta, which grew into a major metropolitan area from its modest beginnings as the southern terminus point for the W&A after Decatur declined the honor.

The extent of the W&A's influence may be debated,

Figure One. United States, 1825–1830

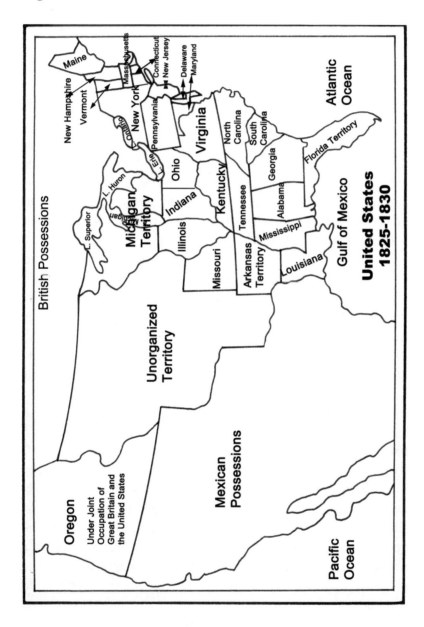

United States
1825-1830

The original thirteen states, in alphabetical order, were: Connecticut, Delaware, Georgia, Maryland, Massachusetts, New Hampshire, New Jersey, New York, North Carolina, Pennsylvania, Rhode Island, South Carolina, and Virginia.

By the time of this map, these states, again in alphabetical order, had become part of the United States (the date of joining is indicated in parentheses following the state): Alabama (1819), Kentucky (1792), Illinois (1818), Indiana (1816), Louisiana (1812), Maine (1820), Mississippi (1817), Missouri (1821), Ohio (1803), Tennessee (1796), and Vermont (1791).

Much of the territory that would ultimately become part of the continental United States remained either unorganized or in the possession of other countries. Already, however, it had become apparent that trade to and from the West would be important to national commercial interests, and it wasn't feasible for all western freight to go down the Mississippi River to the Gulf of Mexico.

For most of the country, there was no transport that did not involve walking or making use of a beast of burden (horse, ox, etc.). There were few public roads, some in the East dating from colonial times, the newest the Cumberland Road that ran west from Cumberland, Maryland, to the Ohio River. The Erie Canal in New York State opened in 1825 and immediately proved its value, but canals could not be constructed just anywhere.

The need for reliable transportation was becoming critical throughout the country.

but its uniqueness cannot be questioned. Of the many nineteenth-century state projects undertaken in the nation, it was probably second in success only to New York's Erie Canal. This was so because the state set for itself a reasonable goal and executed it in a way that ensured it achieved its ends. Many of the projects begun by other states at about the same time were either abandoned incomplete or were so poorly conceived that they failed to fulfill their sponsors' hopes. Georgia was relatively fortunate in its experience with the W&A, and this happy outcome owed much to the fact that it was viewed as the cornerstone of a coherent rail network and not as a standalone project.

When an institution has great subsequent impact, as has the W&A, it is easy to look upon it as always having been inevitable, in form as well as function. Fortunately or unfortunately, such inevitability is rare. Fate preordains few institutions, especially those whose existence requires political action and the expenditure of large sums of money. While the W&A was undeniably the product of chronological, political and economic evolution, it was far from inevitable. Rather, complex situational realities conditioned its creation. Beginning as a general concept, fed by the beliefs and hopes of a few farsighted individuals, and urged by political and economic expedience, what had been a vague idea about general improvement became a specific state project designed to promote the welfare of the people. It was, in effect, an idea that became iron.

The W&A's beginnings lay in the role transportation played in the ability of a region to attract and hold commercial development. Ocean ports had a distinct advantage in this regard, as it was not necessary for them to construct the system that transported people and goods to and from their location (at least via oceangoing traffic), but rather only to build facilities for the docking and unloading of ships. All the major cities of colonial America — Boston, New York, Philadelphia, Baltimore, Charleston, Savannah, etc. — owed their beginnings to geographic locations on or upriver from the Atlantic Ocean. As long as most of the population resided in or relatively near such cities, transportation wasn't enough of an issue to warrant the undertaking of major projects away from the coast. Once greater numbers of people began to move west in post-colonial America, however, the situation changed very quickly.

Westward-moving settlers — who went first into the Northwest Territory (the land between the Great Lakes, the Mississippi, and the Ohio River) and then kept going — wanted not only a dependable way to get their products to market but also to import goods they could not produce themselves. Later settlers expected a way to move west without danger and the undue expenditure of time. Similarly, merchants in the seaboard cities wanted to do business with the rapidly developing West. They wanted to sell goods to Westerners, and they wanted to ship western products abroad and to other cities along the coast.

This required a system of transportation that did not exist apart from rivers snaking through and within states and a few major thoroughfares, like the Great Wagon Road that ran southwest from Philadelphia through Virginia and the Carolinas into Georgia. Most rivers, of course, were not always navigable; and roads — which required ongoing and significant maintenance — sometimes seemed more like ravines than anything we'd recognize today as a reliable way to get from one place to another. As for the extensive network of old Indian trails, this method of land passage was time consuming, expensive and risky to use.

The effect of the patchwork of transport options was to make the Mississippi River route the logical choice for sending western goods to market, which was great for New

Figure Two. Port Cities and Major Roads of Early America

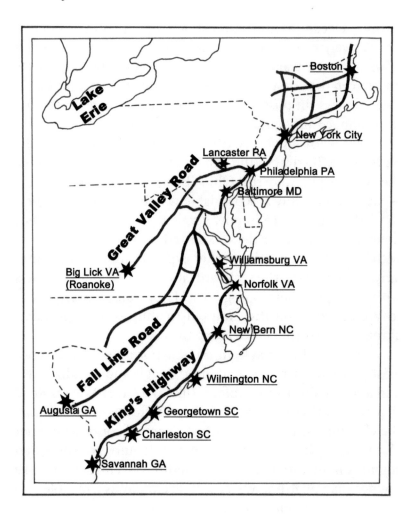

Port Cities and Major Roads
of Early America

The port cities of colonial and post-colonial America owed their early commercial dominance to their positions on or directly upriver from the Atlantic Ocean. The earliest roads (many originating in old Indian trails) developed to connect them or to connect one or more of them to inland areas.

The King's Highway, which was approximately 1,300 miles long, grew from an order of Charles II of England (reigned 1660-1685) who instructed his colonial governors in America to link Charleston, South Carolina, and Boston, Massachusetts. The upper part of this road, which began as the Pequot Path (after the Indians who'd used it for centuries before the arrival of Europeans) was known as the Upper Boston Post Road. The colonial postal service used the route.

The Great Philadelphia Wagon Road passed through the Great Appalachian Valley from Pennsylvania to North Carolina and on to Georgia. This road — divided into the Great Valley Road (terminating in Big Lick Virginia), the Upper Road (terminating in the area of Charlotte, North Carolina), and the Fall Line Road (terminating in Augusta Georgia) — was the route taken by many Early American immigrants, mostly English, Scottish, Irish, and German, to reach the back country of the southern United States. In many places the different manifestations of the road were little more than the Indian trails from which some parts had developed.

The goal of major transportation projects in the nineteenth century was to connect the interior of the rapidly evolving United States with port cities in order to facilitate movement of people and goods in both directions.

Orleans but not for the port cities of the Eastern Seaboard.

Apart from frustrating interurban competition, the situation was hardly suited to the transportation needs of a rapidly growing population wishing to move people and products in an efficient and economical manner. It was clear to all those with a serious interest in trade that commercial activity would be severely limited unless attention was paid to transport. Then, as now, however, the cost of constructing transportation projects was large, the final cost often unknown at the outset, and the political squabbling that accompanied the choice of project and route unending. Private entrepreneurs bold enough to attempt turnpikes, canals, and, later, railroads did not, by and large, have access to capital markets large enough to absorb the cost of their optimistic dreams. This meant that many projects flourished at the outset, only to languish when the realities of cost and limited resources collided. Even had they succeeded, they were often so local and specific in their purpose that privately conceived projects would offer little facilitation for goods or people needing transport for more than a few miles.

Clearly, a more-coherent approach was necessary if American trade could begin to achieve anything approaching its full potential. The goods were there, and so were the markets. The problem was, and remained for decades, that there was no dependable, cost-effective way of transporting supply to demand.

The logical solution, especially from the perspective of businessmen who wanted to move goods and people to or through more than one region, was for the national government to plan and execute a transportation system that would serve all parts of the country in at least a rudimentary way. This was, they argued, an issue that transcended state boundaries.

No one could deny the sense of the argument, but

efforts to interest the national government in internal improvements largely failed. Federal activity was practically nonexistent save for some river clearing, the Cumberland Road (which ran westward from Cumberland, Maryland, connecting the Potomac and Ohio Rivers), and participation in a few small canal projects. In fact, the central government consistently refused to accept any responsibility for a comprehensive transportation network. The most important concession of Congress to the spirit of improvement that had caught hold in the land was its consent in 1824 to the use of Army engineers to survey privately financed roads, canals and, later, railroads. This greatly facilitated individual transportation projects, both private and state-sponsored in nature, because qualified engineers were scarce and this act made available to promoters much of the best engineering talent in the country.

The inactivity of the federal government was offset to some extent by the growing interest in transportation projects throughout the country. New York's Erie Canal, earliest and most successful of the state projects, was making New York City the leading seaport in the country by 1825, the year it was completed. The canal ran 363 miles from Albany on the Hudson River to Buffalo at Lake Erie. By giving freight and passengers traveling either east or west a dependable and more-direct alternative to the tricky Mississippi, the canal filled a great need. So striking was the success of this "big ditch" that it initiated a canal-building boom throughout the country.

Wanting to get the jump on other areas by constructing transportation projects was more than a matter of bragging rights or convenience. It quickly became apparent that regions lacking some reliable method of getting people and goods to, from, and through their area would gradually lose out in the race to become or remain economically successful.

Figure Three. The Historic National Road

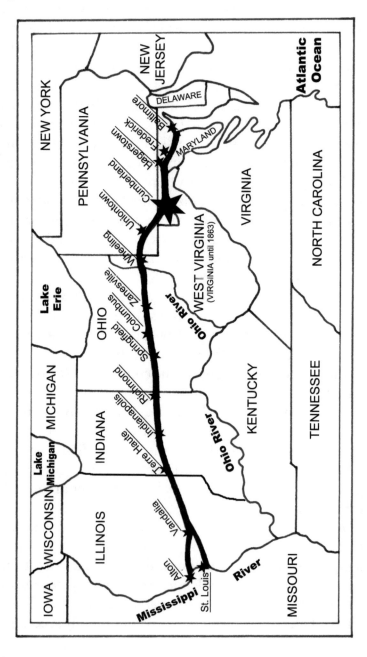

The First Major Improvement
Built by the Federal Government

The Cumberland Road was the first major improvement built by the federal government. Its original goal was to connect the Potomac River, at Cumberland in western Maryland, and the Ohio River at Wheeling in what was then Virginia (later West Virginia). Construction began in Cumberland in 1811, and Wheeling was reached in 1818. At that point, the decision was made to continue westward to St. Louis, Missouri, but intermittent financing delayed reaching this goal for decades. By 1837, the road had reached as far as Vandalia, Illinois, then the capital of Illinois.

Meanwhile, back at the eastern terminus of the road in Cumberland, Maryland, private enterprise financed the construction of a series of turnpikes to connect Cumberland with Baltimore. Once these turnpikes were completed in 1824, it was possible for a traveler capable of paying the tolls, to ride from Baltimore to Cumberland on a reasonably well maintained thoroughfare for the time.

As for the public part of the route, i.e., Cumberland westward, the U.S. Congress had specified it was to be sixty-six feet wide and surfaced in stone covered with gravel. Grades were to be leveled, and bridges were to be stone. These specifications sounded good, but the road in its entirety did not deliver. It's reported that west of Terre Haute, Indiana, no grading was done and stumps were sometimes to be seen on the road bed.

The Cumberland Road, combined with its eastward-to-Baltimore extension, became popularly known as the National Road. Many settlers went west via this route, and it provided a straight passage from the Mississippi River to the East Coast for the movement of products and passengers.

11

Figure Four. The Erie Canal

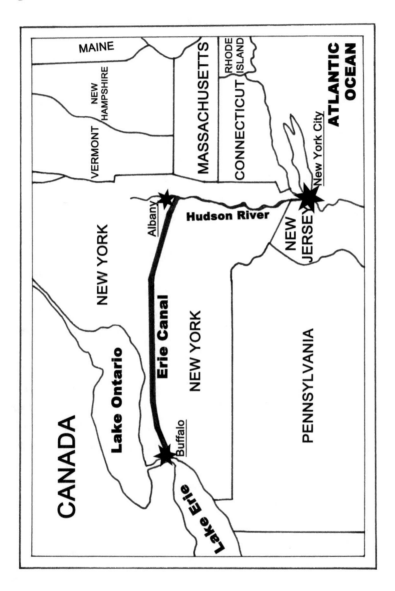

Erie Canal
The Spectacular Success

The Erie Canal, which originates at Buffalo on the northeastern end of Lake Erie and runs 363 miles to Albany, the capital of New York, was built to connect the Great Lakes with the Atlantic Ocean via New York. At Albany, Atlantic-bound traffic leaves the canal to enter the Hudson River to go south to New York City.

Financed by the New York legislature at the urging of Governor DeWitt Clinton, the canal was initially ridiculed as "Clinton's folly." Construction of "Clinton's big ditch" — which was to be forty feet wide and four feet deep, with a towpath to one side — was challenging. The land over which it runs rises about 600 feet from the Hudson River to Lake Erie, necessitating dozens of locks. Much of the route was through hilly, heavily wooded areas that had to be cleared before work could begin. There were major streams and declivities to be crossed with stone aqueducts. perhaps worst of all, the project was plagued with sickness. In one season alone, mosquito-borne malaria killed over 1,000 workers. The effort was not in vain, for the canal was an instant success, quickly achieving the 1.5 million tons of freight anticipated for the first year. When completed, the canal could be used by boats drawing up to three-and-a-half feet of water. These boats were pulled by horses and mules walking on the towpath. It sounds cumbersome, but it revo-lutionized the speed and expense of getting people and goods from west to east and east to west, particularly heavy grains.

Begun in 1817 and finished in 1825, the canal was the only break in the Appalachian Mountains south of the St. Lawrence River and allowed products from the most distant of the Great Lakes to con-tinue their journey by water all the way to New York City, which it quickly made the most-important city in the U.S.

Every state, every city, practically every hamlet had dreams of a canal that would do for it what the Erie had done for New York. Georgia did not escape this fever. Various projects were proposed, usually for the purpose of connecting one of the state's many rivers with another, and local groups were formed to encourage their completion. One of the most ambitious plans was for a canal that would connect the Atlantic with the Gulf of Mexico, bisecting southern Georgia and terminating near Darien.

As elsewhere, however, most of these Georgia schemes remained just that. Canals were costly to construct and not suitable for certain types of terrain. Many authorities, in fact, did not consider them appropriate for the South because their standing waters were believed unhealthy in such warm climates.

The inability to capitalize on the national enthusiasm for canals left the state with an unacceptably limited internal transportation system, consisting of navigable rivers and a few poor market roads. Ambitious businessmen and politicians located in its ports — Savannah, Brunswick and Darien — could, like those of Boston, New York, Philadelphia, Baltimore, and Charleston only watch as New Orleans grew rich from the western trade flowing down the Mississippi River.

Georgia had made some attempts at transportation projects that would nurture trade. From colonial times onward, the state had in fits and starts constructed and maintained a limited market-road network. The most important market-road center in the state, perhaps in the entire Southeast, was Augusta, whose position on the Savannah River at the Fall Line made it a natural clearing point for goods going downriver to Savannah. As with other roads of the time, the lack of a durable surface covering made maintenance difficult. Movement on the roads was slow and uncomfortable. Roadside inns were generally, although not always, primitive and offered little relief for the exhausted traveler.

The improvement project upon which Georgia had spent perhaps the most money was river clearing. The state's extensive river system gave it a better transportation network than most other states enjoyed at the time, but to be useful these rivers had to be kept clear. This was an annual procedure undertaken by local boards financed by the state only after legislative action authorized the amount that could be spent each year.

Other than these efforts at road building, river clearing, and participation in one Savannah canal project, Georgia's early forays into internal improvements were primarily verbal. This was so even though there was a certain amount of support statewide for entry into the improvement field. Local committees began to spring up in the 1820s that requested state assistance in building local works of transportation. Many of these groups wanted canals or roads, but as early as 1826 a committee at Darien expressed a preference for railroads. Darien, a bustling little seaport, was fearful of being eclipsed by its neighbor Brunswick and was eager to provide better transportation to its own facilities.

Legislators and the governor were not ignorant of this growing pressure and had made a response of sorts. By the mid-twenties, Georgia had recruited an English engineer, Hamilton Fulton, and formed a Board of Public Works charged with formulating a comprehensive internal-improvement program for the state. Even before the Board's report was complete, it asked Governor George M. Troup, the Board's president, to write the governor of Tennessee about the desirability of connecting the waters of the Tennessee River with those of the Chattahoochee or the Savannah. There is no record of any answer to this letter, the second of its type written by Troup to the Tennessee chief executive.

The Board of Public Works lasted little more than a

Figure Five. Georgia's Major Rivers

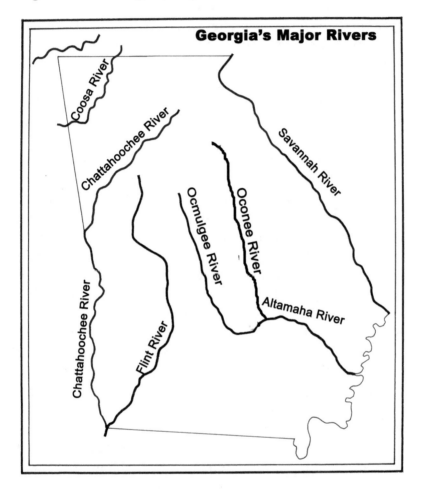

Georgia River System
An Underutilized Natural Resource

Georgia has many rivers. Those shown on this map are the ones that figure most prominently in early talk of transportation development. The Savannah River, approximately 301 miles long, was from the earliest times the most important of the state's waterways because it connected Augusta, a major river port at the termination of the Fall Line Road, with Savannah, the state's leading city.

As for the others, the Coosa flows westward into Alabama, where it was kept navigable for at least part of its length as a means of shipping cotton to market. The Chattahoochee River, roughly 430 miles long, begins in north-central Georgia and terminates in the Apalachicola River which quickly terminates in the Gulf of Mexico. The Flint River, 344 miles long, begins in north-central Georgia and terminates in Lake Seminole just at the Georgia-Florida line. The Altamaha River begins at the confluence of the Oconee and the Ocmulgee Rivers in central Georgia and flows eastward to the Atlantic Ocean — in the nineteenth century it was used for commerce between central Georgia and the coast.

Even in a state as large as Georgia and even allowing for the fact that irregular clearing meant a certain percentage of the rivers were unusable for traffic during some years, these rivers were a great aid to commerce. They shared, however, a significant drawback in that — apart from the Ocmulgee and Oconee, which combined to form the Altamaha — they had no ready means of connecting, which severely limited their usefulness. That's why the Georgia Board of Public Works, formed in 1825, explored the possibility of canals being constructed between two or more of them. Unfortunately, much of the state's terrain did not lend itself to canal building.

Figure Six. Tennessee River and Georgia

Early Dream of Connecting Georgia with Western Trade

Even the biggest promoters of Georgia as a natural commercial leader conceded that the state must attract traffic to and from the West in order to reach its full potential.

Looking at this map, one can see why a connection with the Tennessee River was deemed the likeliest way to do that. This tributary of the Ohio River (it flows into the Ohio at Paducah, Kentucky) is roughly 652 miles long and crosses or borders the states of Kentucky, Mississippi, and Alabama, as well as Tennessee itself. From the beginning of settlement, it was a major route in both directions for people and goods.

What made the Tennessee so tempting for early Georgians ambitious to increase trade to and through the state is that it lies only a few miles from the Georgia-Tennessee border. In the early days, the dream was of a canal that would connect it to either the Chattahoochee or the Savannah. At that time, three obstacles stood in the way: (1) much of northwestern Georgia was legally in control of the Cherokee Indians; (2) there was no guarantee that the governments of Tennessee and Georgia could reach agreement on the connection; and (3) the terrain of northwestern Georgia is mountainous.

Obstacle (1) — the occupation of northwestern Georgia by the Cherokee — was resolved by an agreement between the state and the federal government that resulted in the removal of the Indians. Obstacle (2) did not come to the test until the 1830s, when it was resolved. Obstacle (3), however, was beyond man. Geography made canal construction in this area impractical.

19

year, but in that short time managed to survey various canal and road routes. One particularly interesting exploration was conducted by Chief Engineer Fulton and Wilson Lumpkin, member of the Board and a future governor. Charged with investigating a way of getting goods from the Tennessee River to the Chattahoochee River and on to Savannah, Fulton and Lumpkin set out on horseback from Savannah. Their goal was to determine whether it would be feasible to construct a series of canals to connect the rivers. They reported to the Board that, in their opinion, the terrain would make canal construction too expensive.

In its report to the legislature in November 1826, the Board concluded that any and all internal improvements must serve the agricultural interests of the state. Directing the resources of the state to the acquisition of "foreign trade" would be foolhardy, the Board's report concluded, as the state could not possibly offer sufficient inducements to attract this trade and still make a profit on its improvement investment. Only when the western trade increased in volume and the Cherokee lands in the northwest became part of Georgia would it:

> ...be the obvious interest of the State to construct a suitable line of conveyance to the Tennessee River.

Thus the Board allied itself with the idea that purely local interests must be served before any effort was made to connect the state's transportation system with that of other states.

Upon one point Chief Engineer Hamilton Fulton was adamant. Whatever project was finally selected as worthy of state patronage, he insisted, the promoters of public improvements should concentrate on one important object and see it well done so that the people could quickly realize the benefit. This would secure their continued support for such projects. It was fatal, Fulton felt, to pursue too much and face the possibility of having to abandon all works because of insufficient resources or waning enthusiasm.

Political difficulties and adverse publicity about the chief engineer and his assistant led the legislature to disband the Board before it could prove itself. Its fate was sealed when its supporters did not fight hard to retain it. It may have been that even some adherents were confused by the plethora of projects the Board offered for consideration and were somewhat stunned at the extent of the work needed to give the state a good transportation network. In spite of its short life, the board had a profound effect upon one of its members who later became governor and pushed for both the idea of one important project and a state railroad. Wilson Lumpkin, often called the father of the W&A, owed much of his inspiration to his experience with the Board and his association with Hamilton Fulton.

The press, always enthusiastic about internal improvements, was critical of the Board's dismissal. The *Macon Telegraph* editorialized in November 1826:

> *In all events we hope the State will persevere in the object until something is done to her credit, and not be disheartened because every thing cannot be done at once. Let us begin one thing at a time; and begin something that would be both practicable and useful.*

The Board of Public Works had been a good beginning, but little of immediate use came of it. Causes contributing to Georgia's failure to sustain the Board or to implement any of its recommendations derived from the state's size, its type of economy, its traditional political orientation, and its social makeup.

The state's huge size complicated the antagonism that existed among its various sections. Each area had its own pattern of settlement, distinctive resources, customs, aspirations, and problems. Disagreements between the coast and the interior dated from colonial days. As early as 1772, Lieutenant Governor James Habersham wrote to Governor James Wright about persons settling illegally upon Georgia land just ceded the King by the Indians. Referring to these settlers as "idle people from the Northward, some of whom... are great Villains, Horse thieves &c," Habersham closed his letter with the comment: "You will easily distinguish, that the People I refer to are really what you and I understand by Crackers." Regional antagonism extended to the northern and southern portions of the state as well and was an active force in Georgia politics throughout the nineteenth century. This antagonism had a specific impact on the transportation issue. Money spent by the state to construct an internal improvement would have been viewed by the typical Georgian of 1826 as not only unfairly helping the section in which it was located, but also harming the remainder. There was very little in the way of state pride or consciousness, nor was there any general sense of the indirect benefits that all regions might realize.

Further complicating the regional antagonism was the fact that each part of the state had different priorities related to the primary type of goods produced. Contrary to later popular belief, not all the state was one big cotton bed. Cotton was the predominating crop, especially in the central region, the Southwest and the sea islands, but not the only export. Rice was grown in the coastal swamps and tidelands, and the coast beyond the tidelands produced Indian corn and sugar cane. Sixty miles inland were the pinelands that specialized in timber and the manufacture of tar, pitch, and turpentine. The red, loamy soil of the middle region grew tobacco and all the grains, while the light sandy soil of the Southwest was good for sugar cane. Cherokee Georgia, the northwestern part of the state, consisted mainly of rich valleys producing wheat, corn, Irish potatoes, beans, peas, and onions. Mountainous northern Georgia was the source of valuable minerals — gold, iron, marble, granite, and limestone —making the land here the most valuable in the state between 1830 and 1860.

More than agricultural interests were in play. Savannah and Augusta were well-established commercial centers, and a few progressive businessmen were beginning to consider the advantages Georgia might possess as a manufacturing center. Cotton was still king, but it was clear the crop faced aggressive contenders for the crown.

Just as cotton was not the state's only crop, the planter was not its only law. His wealth and importance influenced many legislative actions, but there was a strong commercial faction whose interests were not always identical to his. The planter's individualism and conservatism often led him to thwart new enterprises, making his influence more negative than constructive. There existed also a large body of rough, independent voters who felt no particular allegiance to either planter or merchant and who were highly suspicious of any state activity likely to raise taxes. As for African-Americans trapped in slavery, they had no vote and influenced the course of state actions only to the degree that those who owned or rented their labor viewed them as a resource for the accomplishment of projects.

Many farmers and planters of the interior viewed large-scale, state-supported improvements as more likely to benefit Savannah and Augusta merchants than themselves. This resentment toward the commercial interests in the older cities arose partly from the fact that occupants of the interior suspected them of an imperial attitude. The coastal merchants wanted the privilege of factoring the farmer's crops and selling him supplies, but seemed little concerned with his special problems.

Aristocrat against Cracker, planter against merchant, farmer against would-be manufacturer — these were often the alignments on state issues. To those seriously concerned with the future of the state as a whole it must sometimes have seemed as if the various factions were more interested in keeping alive the old antagonisms for their own sake than in seeking some point of agreement that would benefit all to one extent or another.

What this meant for transportation was of real concern. The need was critical, but the general political will was weak, which was to be regretted because the issue was capable of resolution. Looked at in one way, the state's transportation problems were simple. Its exports needed a good way to market. Its imports — which included certain types of food-stuffs, hemp, and manufactured goods — required an easy passage to their destination. If a transportation network could be devised which would fulfill these two needs, as well as attract through trade, the state's superior seaports would have an important competitive advantage. That such a net-work could be agreed upon and executed by the state seemed unlikely once the Board of Public Works was disbanded.

Under these circumstances, keeping alive interest in internal improvements was left to individuals, such as Governor Troup, who in 1827 accused the state of ignoring its own potential and implored:

> *I invite your attention again to the subject of Internal Improvements, and to the danger inseparable from a longer postponement of a Judicious System adapted to the wants and resources of the State. It is mortifying to our pride and it will prove ruinous to our interest, that every state in the Union and every state in Europe, advancing in the course of*

improvement, opening communications between the most distant parts of its territory, cheapening its transportation, augmenting its trade and commerce, and cementing the union of its people, give signs of increasing illumination, whilst Georgia with some claims to intelligence and public spirit has not yet executed a solitary work or raised a single monument in illustration of her devotion to the agricultural and commercial prosperity of her people. We must soon withdraw from the rivalry of trade, or share it on the most unequal terms.

For George Troup and others who felt as he did, the next few years must have been particularly frustrating. As Baltimore, Philadelphia and Charleston undertook transportation projects that would connect their port facilities to the West, the Georgia legislature haggled for weeks over bills about river clearing and road maintenance. It seemed as if sectional and political rivalries would keep the state from even attempting to gain that commercial supremacy its advocates predicted for it.

Legislators weren't the only shortsighted politicians in the state. In 1830 Governor George R. Gilmer said that "expensive canals, turnpikes and rail roads" would not suit Georgia, as an extensive transportation system was necessary only where area products were heavy in proportion to their value. Cotton, he proudly pointed out, is light in proportion to its value, and it would be impractical to spend a lot of money to transport it. Interestingly, he felt this proved the superiority of cotton over all other staple products. Concluding his remarks on the subject, he insisted that internal improvements would be a source of complaints, not prosperity.

As to the nature of internal improvements, railroads were becoming an increasingly important option. The Baltimore and Ohio, to run between Baltimore, Maryland, and the Ohio River, was incorporated in 1827 and began operation in 1830 when a line one-and-one-half miles long was opened to the public. This was the start of a railroad boom that in the next thirty years transformed the nature of transportation in the United States. Looking at the newspapers of the time, it's easy to get the impression that any community with ambition was either exploring the possibility of railroad connections or already laying track.

Particularly galling to ambitious Georgians was the fact that the Charleston and Hamburg Railroad in neighboring South Carolina was proving dramatically that it was possible to build a southern railroad in a timely and effective manner. The goal of its builders was to link the seaport of Charleston, 106 miles north of Savannah, with the cotton-growing regions to the west as well as to Augusta, Georgia's busy river port. The first step toward that goal was reached when the Charleston and Hamburg began limited service on Christmas Day 1830, carrying 140 passengers on a six-mile-long line. Once finished, the full route would put the Charleston and Hamburg's terminus a short boat trip away from Augusta, and it took no time at all for the city's business leaders to realize that, once across the river, any goods shipped from Augusta could be in Charleston in short order. That promised profit, but what would almost certainly guarantee more would be if Augusta could itself be the terminus for a more-extensive western route. Augusta businessmen began to look west and northwest, toward Tennessee and Alabama, and contemplate what a rail line from that direction could bring them in traffic.

They were not the only business leaders to recognize the potential. In September 1831, seventy-six delegates from thirty-three Georgia counties assembled in Eatonton in central Georgia to consider the possibility of linking the town with Augusta and its cross-river neighbor, Hamburg, which, as mentioned earlier, was the terminus of the Charleston and Hamburg line. Many of the delegates were prominent businessmen and politicians, and their ambitions for Georgia were on a grand scale. They wanted the state to accept the responsibility for planning and helping to construct not just one project but a system of internal improvements.

Preoccupied by more immediately pressing problems — the Indian question, epidemics, the penitentiary, the college, and the state bank — the legislature failed to act on the suggestions of the Eatonton Railroad Convention.

As state government tried to ignore the transportation issue, the press kept it alive, complaining periodically of Georgia's inability to plan and execute a single improvement project. Pointing out the seriousness of the state's inactivity, the *Southern Recorder* in 1831 admonished sternly:

> *Fickleness in governments as in individuals is equally reprehensible — nay, is far more injurious.*

As usual, state government ignored the press. In fact, had it not been for the well-publicized and ongoing activity of the Charleston and Hamburg Railroad, many years might have elapsed before any concrete action was taken to enter Georgia in the improvement race. Private entrepreneurs, however, responded to this threat and decided they would act, with or without state support. In December 1833, pressured by major private interests, the Georgia legislature chartered three private railroads – the Georgia, the Central of Georgia, and the Monroe.

The Georgia Railroad, initiated in Athens during the summer of 1833, proposed to build a line west from Augusta to Greensboro, Georgia, with a northwest branch to Athens, a westward branch to Madison, and one southwest to Eatonton. The source of support and capital for this project was

Figure Seven. Route of Charleston and Hamburg Railroad

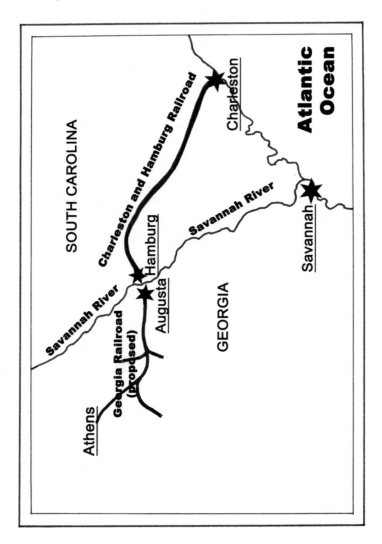

South Carolina Ups the Ante With Charleston and Hamburg Railroad

Charleston merchants seeking to attract more trade from the interior of South Carolina, as well as Augusta, Georgia, formed the South Carolina Railroad & Canal Company in 1827. Their aim was to construct transport that would make irrelevant the swamps and barely passable dirt roads that were then the only way to reach the port from its land side.

The plan was to connect Charleston with cross-state town Hamburg, just across the Savannah River from Augusta, by some combination of railroad and canal. In the event, only rail was used, and the result was attention-grabbing. The line was novel in several ways: (1) it was to be the first common-carrier railroad in the U.S. that was completely steam powered; (2) it operated the first steam train in revenue service in the U.S.; (3) it was 136 miles long, making it the longest railroad in the world at the time; (4) it employed an unusual method of railroad construction in which it was run over swamps that covered much of its route by means of a series of low wooden trestles (later backfilled) so that only straight, dry stretches used the standard crossties-on-the-ground construction; (5) it was able to tap the rich market of Augusta and points west by ferrying passengers across the Savannah River to Hamburg.

The first rail service on any part of the line occurred Christmas Day 1830. The line was completed to Hamburg on October 3, 1833. In anticipation of this completion, businessmen in Athens and Augusta, Georgia, formed a company to construct the Georgia Railroad that would feed passengers and freight into the Charleston and Hamburg. Looking at the map, it's easy to see why Savannah merchants feared ongoing losses of traffic coming downriver from Augusta.

a group of Athens businessmen who planned to create a manufacturing center in the area and wanted an economical, dependable way of transporting their goods to Augusta. As mentioned earlier, one short boat trip across the river, and the goods could be loaded onto the new Charleston and Hamburg line for fast shipment to Charleston.

Already smarting from the challenge posed by Charleston interests that had constructed the railroad to that port, Savannah business leaders took a dim view of this project that would divert from them still more Georgia traffic. Indeed, to Savannahians, the Georgia Railroad appeared almost an extension of the South Carolina road. Georgia's oldest city responded rapidly to this threat, sponsoring a mass meeting in October 1833 to discuss the possibility of a railroad between Savannah, Macon and Columbus. Macon warmly reciprocated Savannah's interest in a connection between the two cities. The result of this agitation was the Central of Georgia Railroad.

The Monroe Railroad originated in Forsyth in 1833 in neighboring Monroe County with the purpose of building a rail line from there to Macon, making it a virtual extension of the Central of Georgia.

The legislature gave all three of these railroads banking privileges to aid them in financing their construction needs. Beyond purchasing some of their stock, the state itself did not commit any form of aid. The projects were, understandably, greeted with much local enthusiasm.

At their inception these three lines were viewed as independent, not as part of any potentially connective system. Their arrangement, however, lent itself well to a relatively simple linkage, a fact that did not long escape proponents of a state transportation project. A state railroad that could connect the lines would benefit all three and the area interests they served, especially if it could also be used to tap the anticipated western traffic.

In spite of the momentum engendered by privately financed rail endeavors, however, the state still refused to undertake any great project of its own even though Governor Wilson Lumpkin suggested that it consider constructing "a central rail road through the entire State" from the coast toward the northwest. Echoing Hamilton Fulton's earlier assertion, Lumpkin said that, to ensure success, all state efforts, support and patronage must be directed to a single project. As discussed earlier, political realities in the state made this difficult.

Finally, a change in Georgia politics created the basis for a somewhat different attitude toward state involvement in transportation projects. In the early 1830s two real political parties emerged in the state: the Union and the States Rights. Unlike the parties of the 1820s, which had been based on personality cults, these groups represented fairly well-defined ideals. The Union was the manifestation of liberal democratic forces. It supported the idea that the state must play a more active role in promoting the welfare of its citizens and its businesses, and thereby attracted many of the most-promising young politicians and businessmen. The States Rights party was more conservative, committed to a balanced budget and economy in state spending. It generally opposed the idea of a larger role for state government in the economic life of the time. Its strongest supporters were planters and other landed interests.

This political transformation did not result in immediate attention being paid to transportation. Preoccupation with more-pressing local concerns and the sensational national issue of Nullification, as well as the Tariff, kept the attention of both parties diverted from the matter of state-supported internal improvements until the mid-1830s. Meanwhile, privately financed rail projects proceeded, albeit more slowly than their backers would have liked.

By 1835 the press had reached a tipping point of frustration. Construction had begun on the Monroe Railroad and the Georgia, and preliminary surveys were being planned for the Central of Georgia. Other states were working frantically on transportation initiatives. The time seemed ripe for the state to begin some significant improvement project of its own. Noting this, the *Southern Banner* pointed an accusing finger at "petty wranglers for local interests" and said that they had kept the state from encouraging and supporting schemes of internal improvement that would have benefited the general interest. Had such support been offered, the *Banner* contended, Georgia would be prosperous and happy, with a higher position in the body of states. Outgoing Governor Wilson Lumpkin shared this opinion, commenting that the "apathy of Georgia" was dangerous.

In 1836 the situation became more intense. On July 4, delegates from various southern states, including Georgia, met in Knoxville, Tennessee to consider possible government-supported railway projects, particularly a line to go from Charleston, South Carolina, to Cincinnati Ohio. The Cincinnati and Charleston Railroad had been proposed at a railroad convention in Cincinnati in August 1835. By several accounts, the conclusions reached at this follow-up Knoxville meeting satisfied most of those attending, but not all. Of the 381 delegates, fifty-five were from Georgia. The Georgians listened as the railroad promoters bragged of what the line would mean to the areas it passed through. They then requested that the charter be amended so as to put a branch of the new line through northern Georgia. The convention agreed. Even so, the Georgia delegates were not among those who left happy, for the agreed-upon route gave them almost nothing they wanted from such a project.

As the Georgians headed homeward from Knoxville,

they discussed the meeting they had just attended. For the first time Georgia political and business leaders were faced with what amounted to an ultimatum in regard to the transportation issue: the state must cooperate with the Cincinnati to Charleston project, initiate a work of its own, or admit it intended to do nothing.

Cooperation with the Cincinnati-Charleston project was distasteful to citizens of southern Georgia because the proposed Georgia branch would cross only the northwestern corner of the state and would divert trade from Savannah to Charleston.

Did that mean the state might finally be ready to enter the internal-improvement game? Given its longstanding resistance to public-transportation projects, getting the Georgia legislature to initiate a work to be owned, controlled and fully paid for by the state still seemed unlikely.

As for doing nothing, that would, believed the Georgia delegates to the Knoxville convention, doom Georgia to the second tier of states in terms of commercial influence. They realized the time had arrived when action of some kind must be taken to direct the fast-growing trade of the West to Georgia. It was true that private interests were actively pursuing railroad activities, but there was no guarantee that the several railroads being planned or already begun would connect in a way that would benefit statewide trade, and none of them were to run anywhere near the Tennessee River or any other trade passage from the West.

Definitive action was required. The disgruntled delegates decided to call all interested Georgians to a railroad convention in Macon in early November 1836. To make certain that as many people as possible were notified, a correspondence committee was chosen whose task it was to contact each county. The invitation issued by this committee described the convention as being called to consider the need and practicality of building a railroad through Georgia to connect the Tennessee River with the Atlantic Ocean.

As the call went forth about the Macon meeting, Governor William Schley had employed Colonel Arthur H. Brisbane, a South Carolina civil engineer, to examine the mountain passes of northern Georgia in connection with possible railroad activity in that area. Brisbane and his assistant, Edward B. White, submitted reports, maps, and estimates on Rabun Gap and alternate passes. This information showed that railroad construction was indeed possible in northern Georgia.

On November 7, 1836, 116 delegates from thirty counties and two railroad companies met at the Macon Methodist Church. On the same day a committee of forty was appointed by the whole convention; to this committee would be referred for action any resolutions adopted by the convention. On November 8, the delegates instructed this committee to report the best means of coordinating the interests of all sections to bring about a connection between the commercial cities of Georgia and the Tennessee River. It's interesting that the committee's report was ready the next day (or about the length of time it took committee members to retrieve it from their cases). The report emphasized the committee's awareness of the importance of the proposed project to the permanent prosperity of Georgia:

> When a commercial intercourse shall once be opened by means of a judiciously devised system of Rail Roads between the several leading places of trade in Georgia and the navigable waters of the Tennessee River, it requires not the gift of prophecy to enable us to foresee that a powerful impulse and vast expansion will be immediately imparted to all our resources of greatness and social improvement.

Completion of the railroad, the report contended, would

open to Georgia the trade of the West to the Rocky Mountains and the trade of the North as far as the Great Lakes.

The writers of the report, determined to take no chances, even called upon George Washington's endorsement. Reminding the delegates of the national government's early interest in connecting the Ohio River with the Atlantic, the report stated:

> *Such an idea, deliberately entertained, and earnestly patronized by the Father of his country, could not fail to sink deep in the public mind.*

Summarizing the great works of improvement undertaken in other states, the report reiterated Georgia's advantageous location in relation to the West and asked:

> *Will the people and government of Georgia slight so benign and magnificent an overture of nature in their favor? Will they refuse to lead their own concurrence and co-operation to effect a complete fulfilment of the grand destiny which a partial Providence has put so clearly and easily within their achievement?*

Many of Georgia's problems, social and economic, might be solved by completing a good transportation system. Furthermore, the report continued, the public approved the idea and the state could afford it. In view of the state's favorable financial situation, the committee recommended that the portion of the line from the Tennessee River to the Chattahoochee should be constructed and financed by the state and that the state should aid companies willing to construct branches to connect its line with those already existing or proposed.

Even at the Macon convention, there was some resistance to the state's constructing the line, but a motion to

Figure Eight. Proposed State Railroad and Early Georgia Railroads

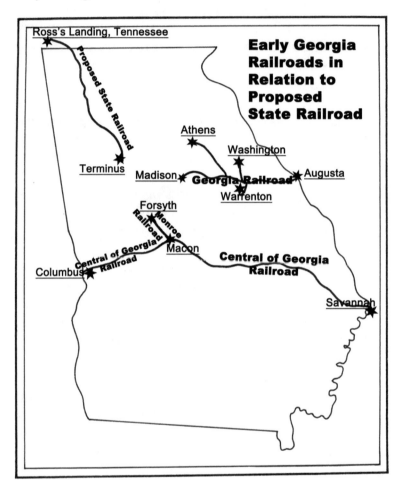

State Railroad Intended
To Serve Two Functions

*Looking at this map of major Georgia railroads being planned
or already under construction in 1836 shows why the delegates to
the Macon Convention thought it made sense for the state to construct and control a railroad. It would serve two functions that had
long been a dream of politicians and businessmen frustrated by
the state's reluctance to undertake a great project. First, it would
connect the central part of the state to a port on the Tennessee River,
a gateway to western trade. Second, it could easily be connected by
branches to the Georgia, Monroe, and Central of Georgia Railroads, thereby creating a statewide rail network. Achieving these
two goals would give the state railroad both commercial and
political relevance.*

*Although the precise route (and the location of Terminus) would
be determined only after the final surveys, everyone knew the line
would run somewhere in this area.*

*It's difficult to believe the state had not done something along these
lines earlier. It wasn't a matter of money, for there was plenty in the
treasury to undertake such a railroad. Rather, there was so much
political infighting, particularly (but not entirely) within the States
Rights Party, that it was hard to get enough votes in the state
legislature to pass a major public project that seemed to benefit one
region at the expense of others. In fact, the stalemate over railroad projects was one of the reasons several railroad men — most
notoriously William Washington Gordon of Savannah, the Central
of Georgia's president — ran for office and became legislators for
a term. With their support, the the bill to construct a state railroad
— to be known as the Western & Atlantic — finally became law in
December 1836.*

strike that part of the report was defeated. The supporters of state involvement had come too far and were too close to their goal to be so easily sidetracked.

It was agreed that a small committee would present to the legislature the results of the convention and would exert every influence to see that the state adopted the plan. It was anticipated that this would be made easier by the presence of William Washington Gordon (president of the Central of Georgia) and other powerful railroad men, who were — as mentioned earlier — sitting in the legislature for this one term expressly to promote railroad interests.

Luckily for the proponents of this idea, the Union party — the more progressive of the two leading parties — had control of the legislature and held the governorship, which ensured a generally favorable atmosphere in which the pro-railroad proposals would be presented. Even so, approval was by no means guaranteed. There remained powerful interests in the legislature opposed to the whole concept of public transportation projects. There were other legislators who would not like the route proposed, arguing instead for one running through their localities. Even those legislators who approved in principle of public-transportation projects and who did not object to the route, might have second thoughts about the scope of the expenditure to which the state would be committing.

Whatever the individual attitudes or motivations of its members, the governing body that was to be faced with approval or rejection of the Macon plan found itself at a crossroads. As mentioned earlier, the state of Georgia had dabbled in internal improvements since colonial times. Its involvement, however, had been of the hand-to-mouth variety, as likely to be stopped by one legislature as it was to be reinitiated by the next. Also, the projects had been largely of a maintenance nature. If the money were cut off one year, this did not necessarily mean that monies spent in previous years had been wasted, only that this particular year a certain number of rivers would not be cleared or roads repaired. Obviously, the railroad project represented something quite different. In the first place, it would cost a great deal of money in a short time frame. Also, once it was begun, turning back would mean the virtual loss of what had been spent, for the primary value of the proposed line was its connective character. Denied this, there was little justification for the line's existence. Incomplete, the railroad would serve only the settlers straggling into the northwest as the Indians moved out. There might be much future social gain, but little immediate commercial advantage.

In spite of these financial considerations, circumstances forced the legislature to give serious consideration to the Macon plan. For one thing, enthusiastic publicity given the improvement projects of other states made it clear that competition for trade supremacy would not be won by the fainthearted. For another, intensification of the press campaign for a state improvement kept the issue before the people.

Another consideration was that the political party in power, the Union, needed the prestige that would result from a spectacular project capable of generating popular enthusiasm and of providing an impressive amount of patronage to dispense.

Perhaps even more important, a legal and physical obstacle to development in northwestern Georgia had been eliminated with the passage by the Twenty-First Congress of the Indian Removal Act of 1830. This act — which many view as a particularly disgraceful injustice, albeit one that simplified development — called for the forcible ejection of Indians from eastern states and their resettlement west of the Mississippi River. This left the valuable lands the Indians had occupied in northwestern Georgia ready for use.

Most important, the state could afford to undertake a grand project. Financially, it was in excellent shape, and there was also the possibility of a surplus revenue distribution from the federal government.

Suddenly, what had once seemed sensible hesitation to involve the state in what many felt should be private enterprise began to appear overly cautious. Georgia might be reluctant to act, but clearly other states were not. The situation could be ignored no longer. Civic pride and fear of economic isolation combined to make 1836 a year of decision.

Adding to the sense of urgency was the fact that the legislature had given much consideration to the topic of railroads in recent months, specifically to lines that would be built by private interests. In the legislative session ending at the close of December 1836, for example — apart from the act authorizing the W&A, which we'll consider shortly — the following railroad-related acts were passed and then assented to by Governor William Schley.

> • An Act "To authorize and empower the Brunswick and Florida Rail Road Company, to construct a branch from the said road, from any point on said road, to any point on the Flint and Chattahoochee rivers. (And) That for the purpose of completing the Brunswick and Florida Rail Road, and the branch, hereby authorized to be constructed, the capital stock of said company, may be increased to any sum not exceeding five million of dollars."

> • An Act "To alter and amend an act, entitled 'an act to incorporate the Chattahoochee Rail Road Company,' passed the 21st day of December, 1835, and to give to said Company, banking powers and privileges."

> • An Act "To grant Thomas Spaulding, Esq., Lewis A. Bond, Charles Day, James R. Butts and Alexander Shotwell, the

right of constructing a Rail Road from the Flint, to the Chattahoochee river, with certain privileges."

• *An Act "To amend the acts incorporating the Georgia Rail Road and Banking Company, and the Central Rail Road and Banking Company of Georgia."*

• *An Act "To incorporate a Rail Road Company, to be called the Middle Branch Rail Road Company, for the purpose of constructing a Rail Road, from Madison, in Morgan county to the Chattahoochee river, by way of Covington, in Newton county."*

• *An Act "To amend the charter of the Monroe Rail Road Company, incorporated for the purpose of constructing a Rail Road from the City of Macon to the Town of Forsyth, in Monroe county; to extend the route of said Road in a North-western direction; to alter and change the name of said Company; and to confer on said Company, banking powers and privileges."*

• *An Act "To amend an act, entitled an act, to amend an act, to incorporate the Georgia Rail Road Company, with power to construct a Rail or Turnpike Road from the city of Augusta, with branches extending to Eatonton, Madison, in Morgan county, to Athens; to be carried beyond those places at the discretion of said company; to punish those who may willfully injure the same; to confer all corporate powers necessary to effect said object; and to repeal an act, entitled an act, to authorize the formation of a company, for constructing a Rail road from the city of Augusta to Eatonton, and thence westward to the Chattahoochee river, with branches thereto, and to punish those who may injure the same; to alter and change the name of said company and to give to said company, banking powers and privileges, passed 18th December, 1835."*

> • An Act *"to incorporate the Saint Marys and Columbus Rail Road Company."*

Clearly, those "one-term railroader" legislators who'd come to Macon to promote private railroad interests had used their time well.

That brings us to the act that was to give birth to the W&A, the great public railroad project. Assuming that the issue could no longer be ignored, why should the state sponsor a railroad to the northwest rather than a railroad elsewhere or a canal or additional roads? The answer was obvious. The route had two advantages. Its northwestern terminus, just over the state line at the Tennessee River, would allow the state access to the longed-for western markets. Its southern terminus, in north-central Georgia, could be made to unite the state's private railroads that were being planned or were already begun. In that way, the proposed public railroad could be said to serve the state and not just parts of the state.

Speed was of the essence, supporters reminded the legislature. If the connection were to give Georgia an appreciable advantage, it must be made soon, before other southern states successfully tapped the western market and established trade patterns that would be difficult to alter. The route's internal advantages were less measurable, but the road would give the people their first true statewide transportation system, which could only be an asset.

As for the choice of a railroad to provide this internal and external link rather than a canal or a road, the train was no longer an experimental novelty and offered advantages that canals and roads did not. The earlier forms of transportation had proven too dependent upon elements over which man had no control, particularly weather and terrain. What was needed was a transportation method that could be constructed just about anywhere, operated consistently, and be more easily maintained. Railroads met these criteria. Their overriding advantage is that they can go almost anywhere men want to put them. This was an especially potent factor in the choice of the railroad for the route through north-western Georgia because the mountainous terrain in this area was highly impractical for canals.

One question that arose during the debates over the W&A was why should Georgia commit itself to just one large project? Why should it not disperse its interest among sev-eral as other states had done? It was a matter of focus and resources, supporters of the Macon plan said. They reminded the legislature that informed opinion in the state in the 1820s and 1830s had emphasized the need for concentration on one big improvement. They also reminded legislators of the danger of attempting too much at once. Wilson Lump-kin, for example, had continually harped on this idea, both as a member of the Board of Public Works and as governor. The subsequent experience of other states, particularly Indi-ana, bore out the insistence of transportation experts on this point. Several states planned and actually began construc-tion on overly ambitious programs only to be forced to aban-don them half finished for lack of funds and public interest.

Opponents of the Macon plan wondered what could Georgia expect if the plan were executed. Some argued such a work would unfairly increase the value of land along its route and augment the population of northwestern Georgia at the expense of other parts of the state.

Supporters of the Macon plan predicted a revitalization of all aspects of Georgia life. Commercial interests hoped for new prosperity. State boosters argued the plan would make Georgia the leading southern state. Wilson Lumpkin pre-dicted that the success of the plan would enhance the wealth of every Georgian and would increase the value of the railroad stock the state already held in private lines.

These expectations seemed reasonable. The line would greatly increase the state's potential as a commercial center and would encourage the use of Savannah port facilities by Westerners who might otherwise ship to Charleston or New Orleans. All of the state would receive some benefit, direct or indirect, and agricultural as well as commercial interests would be served because planters and farmers would gain a faster, more dependable way of getting their crops to market and of importing necessary equipment and goods. While it was true that the private railroads would be more important to the planter as a transportation device, it was felt that state activity in building the proposed line would encourage the private companies to complete their own lines more rapidly.

Cautious legislators seeking theoretical justification for putting the state into the railroad business could find it in the influential eighteenth-century economist, Adam Smith, who felt that one of the proper functions of government was the creation of a good internal-transportation system. Also, contemporary transportation authorities felt the state government was in the best position to plan, promote, and execute works of improvement. After all, the state government should know conditions and needs more thoroughly than any other institution, and its legislative power enabled enactment of any necessary measures to achieve its ends. That last consideration — the ability of the state legislature to enact laws to support railroad activity — was more important than it might appear today. Railroads, like all new fields of endeavor, brought special challenges in regard to the organization and conduct of planning, financing, purchasing rights of way, construction, and operation. Much of this required changes in or addition to existing law that only the legislature could implement.

A pragmatic reason for state entry into the improvement field was the scarcity of private capital all over the United States. This scarcity was due primarily to the rapidly increasing demand for money as the West was opened. As a public borrower, the state could obtain money at more-favorable interest rates than a private concern. In addition, the English and European money market was an eager purchaser of state railroad bonds at this time. Thus, if the state's existing financial reserves proved inadequate to complete the project, it should have little difficulty in finding sufficient funds elsewhere.

Another important consideration regarding a railroad through northwestern Georgia was the reluctance of private corporations to construct an improvement that was to go through comparatively empty country. Clearly, a line across the previously undeveloped northwestern part of the state was needed if Georgia interests hoped to tap western markets via the Tennessee. At the same time, it might be years before adequate connections were made to give the line through traffic, and there was little prospect of enough local traffic to generate profit before that time. This improvement, at least for the first few years, was clearly to be classed as of the general-advantage variety and not as a commercial venture that could be judged by normal business standards. Few private enterprises could justify such far-thinking altruism. If the state didn't build the critical connection, who would?

Even assuming private capital was willing and able to construct the line, should it be allowed to? There was throughout the nation a certain disinclination to permit private corporations control of a vital work of transportation. In Georgia, distrust of one private company's owning this vital link with the West may have been an especially potent undercurrent. If the Georgia Railroad owned or controlled the proposed connection, for example, it might divert all traffic over its lines to Augusta and thence to Charleston, bypassing Savannah and thereby defeating part of the improvement's purpose. Likewise, the Central of Georgia might be tempted to discriminate against the Georgia Railroad if in a position to do so. Rather than risk the possibility of future discord on this account, it seemed simpler to let the state control the link. In any event, at this time little conflict existed between public and private endeavor. So much needed to be done in the state and the resources of private enterprise were so relatively limited that public sponsorship of improvements almost inevitably redounded to the benefit of private interests. Private concerns rarely opposed state activity for this reason.

With all this in mind or perhaps with none of it even thought of, for such is the way of politics, the Georgia legislature of 1836 was faced with the responsibility of accepting or rejecting the Macon plan. After years of discussion and hesitation regarding the state's proper role in internal development, the General Assembly now had a clear choice. The committee from the Macon Convention had presented a reasonable plan that, if passed, would commit the state government to the railroad business.

There was no ambiguity in the Macon plan, no vague hope that the state government would assist some unspecified project or projects at some future date. Instead, the plan proposed the state government should begin immediately to survey and construct a railroad from the Tennessee River to the Chattahoochee, providing full financing and retaining full control and supervision. In addition, the state should substantially assist in the construction of the connecting branches outlined in the plan.

In the event, a bill, corresponding almost entirely with the Macon plan, was introduced into the Georgia House on November 29, 1836, by William Washington Gordon of Savannah. The measure had already been reviewed by the internal-improvement committee, of which Gordon was a member.

The full title of the Act was precise in its wording.

> *To authorize the construction of a Rail Road communica-*
> *tion from the Tennessee line, near the Tennessee river, to*
> *the point on the Southeastern bank of the Chattahoochee*
> *river, most eligible for the running of branch roads, thence*
> *to Athens, Madison, Milledgeville, Forsyth, and Columbus;*
> *and to appropriate monies therefor.*

That the bill was to serve as a plan of action was made clear by its inclusion of specifics — where it was to run, what its construction could cost annually, how it was to be surveyed, how expenditures were to be accounted for, who was in charge of disbursements, how right-of-way purchases were to be handled, what was to happen when the route of the railroad intersected with public or private roads, the penalties for hindering construction or for afterwards damaging the railroad, how the construction of branch lines was to be encouraged and subsidized, and the frequency of the chief engineer's reports to the governor. The bill also named the new enterprise:

> *And be it further enacted by the authority aforesaid, That*
> *said Rail Road shall be known and distinguished as the*
> *Western and Atlantic Rail Road of the State of Georgia.*

After two more readings, much discussion, and numerous attempts to have the bill amended or tabled, it was passed virtually intact by the House on December 10 by a vote of 100-54. On December 12 reconsideration of the measure was moved and rejected 75-66.

The same day, notice was read in the Senate that the House had passed the bill, and it was read for the first time in the Senate. After a second reading, the bill followed much the same course in the upper house as it had in the lower. Various amendments were offered and rejected, but the result was the same. The bill passed as read December 16 by a vote of 46-34. Motion for reconsideration was rejected 47-32 on December 17.

As roll-call votes were recorded in both Senate and House, it is possible to break down the vote and provide a simple analysis of support and opposition by county delegation. These delegations consisted of one senator and from one to five representatives. Only one delegation did not vote.

Of the eighty-nine county delegations that voted on the W&A bill, thirty-six supported it unanimously, twenty-six opposed it unanimously; and twenty-seven divided their votes. A study of census statistics reveals a clear pattern in the vote. Population density, distance from the proposed W&A route, manufacturing variety, and per capita commercial investment appear to have been influential factors in the passage of the W&A bill. Counties supporting the measure had a much greater population density, a greater diversity of manufacturing activities, and an impressively larger per capita commercial investment than those who opposed the measure and those who divided their vote. Those counties most distant from the proposed route and — except for certain key areas such as Savannah, Macon and Columbus — most unlikely to receive any benefit, direct or indirect, from the W&A for some time provided the most-consistent opposition to the bill. Heaviest support for the bill came from northwestern Georgia, through which the railroad would run, and from the large commercial centers.

From this analysis, it is clear that those areas already relatively highly developed provided the strongest support for the W&A and that those less developed opposed it. But, whatever the motives of the individual legislators and whether or not they had voted rationally according to the economic interests of their counties, as a body they had taken the first big step. The state of Georgia had at last begun its Great Undertaking.

The fear that gripped the visionaries who felt the W&A was essential to the state's future was that the 1837 legislature would reconsider and scratch the project. This apprehension dictated the frantic activity undertaken on the W&A during 1837. As William Schley, the Unionist governor, confided to the Central of Georgia's W.W. Gordon in a letter in January 1837:

> *I am very anxious to commence the work as soon as possible, in order that I may have the surveys completed and a large portion of the route under contract before the meeting of the next Legislature. In fact, I desire to spend all the money I can, lawfully and economically, this year, that there may be no danger of an abandonment of this great work, so honorable to the State.*

Before Schley could do anything, he had to find a chief engineer to supervise the survey and let the construction contracts. To create more popular interest in and support for the W&A, Schley was determined that the man chosen be a leader in his field, well known and respected.

This hope was easier to hold than to realize. Competition was brisk for good engineers in 1837 because of the large number of improvement projects underway throughout the nation. Also, many engineers did not want to move south because of the area's reputed unhealthiness. Trying to assuage the fears of one man on this point, Schley wrote:

> *The country in which you will be engaged is one of the finest climates on the globe, and you will run no risk of bilious fever.*

49

Perhaps more of a drawback than the state's climate was its mania for economy, as salaries commanded by the best engineers generally ranged from $6,000 to $12,000 a year ($146,340 to $292,685 in 2014 dollars), more than Georgia was willing to pay. The large salaries created another potential problem in that they attracted imposters, a possibility that posed an additional hazard for a conscientious governor looking for a good engineer. The country was so large, projects so numerous, and the number of trained engineers so small that it was unlikely a fraud would be exposed until too late. This meant extreme care had to be exercised in Schley's search for the right man.

Governor Schley was by nature cautious. He knew little of engineering himself and was smart enough to realize his deficiency. His first act after passage of the W&A bill was to contact various railroad men and engineers around the state for recommendations of a suitable engineer. He received many names, and his subsequent correspondence with one engineer after another proved one of his most frustrating experiences as governor.

Schley's first choice was William Gibbs McNeill, a West Point classmate of W.W. Gordon's, but he could not bring himself to accept McNeill's plan to supervise the project from New York while an assistant did the actual on-site work. Unfortunately, almost three months' correspondence was necessary before the two men realized their differences were irreconcilable. Meanwhile, Schley had turned down the services of at least one other engineer, Andrew Alfred Dexter, who had worked on the Charleston and Hamburg Railroad, the Mobile and Tennessee, and the Montgomery and West Point surveys. The governor also found himself involved in an acrimonious exchange of letters with Colonel Arthur Brisbane of South Carolina, who had surveyed the mountain passes the previous autumn and had expected to be appointed chief engineer as a matter of right. The tactful Schley promised Brisbane the post of first assistant and tried to smooth his ruffled pride.

Schley's second choice for chief engineer was John J. Abert, a Colonel in the topographic corps. Abert, a competent man but unwilling to take the job for less than $10,000 a year, was not under serious consideration for long.

Abert's own recommendation for the job was Lieutenant Colonel Stephen H. Long, whom he described as being "one of the most amiable of men, as well as one of the best informed of our officers — particularly well versed in the properties of Rail Roads." Abert's description of Long's qualifications was, if anything, an understatement. Long had been the chief engineer on the pioneering Baltimore and Ohio Railroad. Since J. Edgar Thomson, chief engineer of the Georgia Railroad, also enthusiastically recommended Long, Schley felt he was a safe choice and engaged him at the end of March 1837, more than three months after passage of the W&A bill.

Justifying this delay in a letter to J. Edgar Thomson as being occasioned by his determination to obtain a "celebrated" engineer, Schley wrote:

> Much is due to public opinion, and therefore I have endeavored to avail myself of the services of such as had high reputation for attainments in the profession.

In Stephen H. Long, Schley had found the right man. Born in Hopkinton, New Hampshire, Long matriculated at Dartmouth, teaching for a few years after getting his degree. He entered the army in 1814 at the age of thirty as a lieutenant in the Engineer Corps. For the next two years, he was professor of math at West Point. In 1816, he transferred to the Topographic Engineers with the rank of Major and began a career of exploration that would make him one of the foremost figures in the discovery of the West and see a high peak in the Rocky Mountains named for him. From 1827 to 1830 he supervised the survey of the Baltimore and Ohio Railroad. In 1829, he wrote the first original treatise on railroad building published in the United States. In the intervening years he had surveyed various railroad routes.

Long brought to the W&A the most-impressive credentials in this new and sometimes difficult business of railroad building. That he continued to exercise his expertise effectively in Georgia may be seen from the fact that the entire profession copied the system of curves he devised for the W&A and that he was able to patent his method of trestle-and-bridge construction for the line.

As an assistant to Long, Schley engaged the previously disappointed Colonel Brisbane. For his other two assistants, Long chose W.S. Whitwell and Thomas Stockton.

As he waited for his engineers to appear, Schley gave J. Edgar Thomson permission to recruit the surveying parties Long would need. Thomson, as chief engineer of the Georgia Railroad, was happy to oblige Schley, demonstrating the close relationship between the management of the existing railroads and the political administration.

As would be the case today, Schley found himself instantly deluged with letters and visits from men or groups who sought to advance their individual fortunes or careers by association with the W&A project. Schley, a very punctilious individual, had much the same answer for all. He was not yet authorized to make such moves and, in any event, the time had not come to send an agent to Europe to buy iron or to employ a general agent. Schley's reply was always polite and almost always a refusal.

One of his more-insistent correspondents was S.D.

Jacobs, president of the Highwassee Railroad, a proposed line which would run very close to the projected termination of the W&A in Tennessee. The Georgia Railroad management had apparently at some point promised Jacobs a connection with the W&A, yet the route proposed by the legislature would not accomplish this union. Attempting to convince Schley of the advantages the W&A would gain by connection with the Highwassee, Jacobs pointed out the strategic location of his railroad and the large area it would serve in eastern Tennessee. Jacobs rather fulsomely complimented Georgia on its vision in beginning this great work to tap traffic on the Tennessee, but reminded Schley that navigation on the river was limited to a few months of the year and that this would severely restrict the usefulness of the W&A. Referring to rumors he had heard that the state had contemplated extending the railroad over the Tennessee River across Tennessee to Nashville, Jacobs made a brave show of pretending to be uninterested:

> *Let it not be conceived that we are opposed to the extension of your road to the Tennessee River (and beyond)... provided you also unite with us. We have no objections to that improvement, as we are satisfied it can do us but little if any injury; our only object is to endeavor to convince your Excellency, that if you cannot construct both roads, the interests of your State will be much more certainly, effectually and immediately subserved by uniting with the Highwassee Rail road.*

Jacobs's nonchalance was somewhat marred by his subsequent admission that unless the W&A chose to connect with the Highwassee his railroad would be hard pressed to acquire the necessary capital for completion. Although Jacobs pulled out all the stops, Schley stood firm, replying that the legislature had designated the approximate terminus of the road in Tennessee and that if this terminus were to be changed it must be by legislative action. If, however, Jacobs would like to extend his road to unite with the W&A, Georgia would have no objection.

Throughout this frustrating time in early 1837 as he waited for Long to make the journey from the North, Schley's enthusiasm for the project was kept alive by his conviction that the railroad would mean much both to the state and to the Union Party. Helping bolster this belief were encouraging messages from various leaders around the state. William Dearing of the Georgia Railroad, for one, predicted a glorious future for the W&A:

> It will be hailed by unborn multitudes as one of the most important events in the history of Georgia, if it should be properly and judiciously prosecuted to completion; and I need not say that this great work belongs to you and your administration. This great enterprise, when completed, will be to Georgia what the great Canal in New York is to that state. Georgia must become her own importer, not only for her own wants, but for the wants of much of the west. Georgia has the only natural Channel of communication connecting the Atlantic with the west; and this Rail Road will secure the connection.

The ever-active W.W. Gordon stopped labors on the Central of Georgia long enough to write from Savannah:

> Public feeling is enlisted to the utmost in this matter...If this work be begun with spirit and executed with vigor, it will enable us to recover as a party, all that we have lost by our supineness and in this and most other sections of the State, it will probably be the test question.

In spite of such buoying messages, Schley's anxiety

increased daily as Long failed to appear when expected in late April. Long finally reached Milledgeville, the state capital, on May 9, 1837. He and Schley immediately had a misunderstanding as to the terms on which he had been engaged to act as chief engineer. It was decided that Long would undertake the post for six months' recompense of $2500 and permission to return north to make arrangements about his family in New Hampshire. His subsequent compensation was to depend on legislative action. Like most Army engineers employed on private assignments, Long was obliged to continue to conduct a certain amount of Army business, and Schley agreed to this. A contract was drawn up embodying these terms and declaring that:

> *William Schley, on behalf of the State of Georgia, agrees to constitute and appoint the said S.H. Long, Chief Engineer of the said Rail Road, with full powers, privileges and authority to survey, locate and construct said Rail Road and its several appendages, as provided for by the law of December 21, 1836.*

After so many bad experiences with poor communication, Schley took no further chances and drew up a "Project of Instructions" for his new engineer, setting forth specifically Long's duties and the restrictions and privileges conferred upon the chief engineer by the act creating the railroad. The terms were generous. Long was to have:

> *...full power and authority to treat with any owner of land... through which said Rail Road may be cut or constructed, or from which, any timber or other materials may be taken for the construction of said Railroad, and to fix and agree upon a compensation for the same.*

Long was to have carte blanche in the obtaining of

not only supplies, but men, the only stipulations being that the sums spent not total more in aggregate than the funds the legislature voted and that accurate records be kept. The most-serious responsibility placed upon the chief engineer, to which Long strenuously objected, was that he must be the judge as to whether or not individual contracts entered into in connection with the W&A were in the best interest of the state of Georgia. Long felt the other duties of his job kept him too busy to perform such a function properly and that, in any event, this was not a proper matter for an engineer to decide. Schley agreed and began efforts to have this provision changed.

It was late May before Long began his initial reconnaissance of the proposed route. Understanding the governor's nervousness as to time, Long sent encouraging letters every few days as he traveled. He was soon joined by the men who would head the exploring parties.

Having decided on a really thorough instrumental survey, Long next set up three separate field parties, each consisting of a principal assistant engineer, a sub-assistant engineer, three surveyors, two rodmen, two chainmen, two axemen, one purveyor, one wagoner, one cook, and one "active lad." These parties were given complete instructions by Long, who left in late July to return north to his family.

Letters written by Schley during the spring and early summer of 1837 refer repeatedly to illnesses in his eyes. To his apparent physical discomfort was added what seemed to him the agonizing slowness of the survey. To hurry it along, Schley himself made two inspection trips to the area.

Meanwhile, the citizens of Ross's Landing, Tennessee, legislature-designated terminus of the W&A, had learned of the Highwassee's attempt to have the terminus changed to a point nearer the end of its own line. In a memorial to Schley, a concerned committee protested any change. Only by locating the railroad where the legislature had said it should go — namely, to Ross's Landing — could Georgia hope to tap the western trade, or so the good citizens of that hamlet insisted. Should Georgia see fit to follow its original plan, the group predicted, the cities of Augusta, Savannah and Brunswick would vie in importance with the cities of the North and a prosperous new city would surely spring up on the Tennessee River. (In this, they were correct. The site is now known as Chattanooga.)

In his usual calm fashion, Schley assured the people of Ross's Landing that the route of the railroad would not be changed unless the legislature so decided or unless it proved impossible to construct the line as proposed. Schley was very sensitive to charges that favoritism might be practiced in the location of the railroad. This fear was why he supported Long in his decision to survey several possible routes between the Chattahoochee and the Tennessee, even though this meant the survey would take longer. Such thoroughness, Schley wrote Long, was necessary:

> ...in order that the people, who feel a deep interest in the matter, may be satisfied that equal justice has been done to all; and that the location finally determined on is the 'shortest and most practicable route,' that could be obtained to effect all the objects contemplated by the Legislature.

If all this seems a borderline paranoid, it must be placed in the context of the times. The psychological aura surrounding internal improvements was such that many people, perhaps most, felt that inclusion on the route of a railroad or canal was tantamount to a happy ending or, rather, a happy beginning, an introduction to new prosperity. Location of such improvements was, therefore, a highly charged emotional affair and a matter of grave importance.

After years of agitating for a state improvement, the press played it cool during the first important year of the W&A. Perhaps the general press reaction was best expressed by a cynical editorial in the *Southern Recorder* in January 1837, just one month after the W&A bill was passed:

> *It seems, somehow or other, to have been deemed quite suf-*
> *ficient to have traced out canals and railroads upon maps,*
> *trumpeted forth the respective advantages in a few florid*
> *paragraphs and meetings, and then to have left the rest*
> *to posterity.*

The press, in other words, would believe in the state railroad only when it heard the toot of the train. Most mentions in the Georgia press in 1837 confined themselves to routine reporting of the progress of the survey.

For once, however, media pessimism was ill founded. In spite of Long's continued absence, ten miles of the road was located and ready for contract by October 6, 1837. It had been Schley's purpose to commit the state beyond any feasible point of repudiation, and he had succeeded. Unfortunately, his success may have been gained at the expense of his political career, for he lost his bid for a second term as governor in October. The *Darien Telegraph* described Schley as "truly a man without reproach," and much of the state press and many of the state's politicians and businessmen agreed. Yet he lost a close race to George R. Gilmer, governor in 1831-1832. One of the issues was the amount of time Schley devoted to the W&A project, but this was probably not nearly so decisive a factor in his defeat as his careful (tight-fisted, some said) handling of claims against the state from men who had served in the late Indian wars. A split in the Union Party between liberals and the conservative party machine kept him from having his organization's full support. Perhaps even more important was the panic of 1837, which was of course beyond Schley's control and certainly not of his making. Bad times often signal a change in administration.

The W&A itself was not an issue in the campaign except that some of the press feared Gilmer's election on the basis of his once-expressed belief that Georgia did not need a state railroad. These fears proved groundless. Gilmer evidently prosecuted the work with almost as much vigor as Schley.

Schley had not fulfilled his desire to have the road completely surveyed and under contract by late 1837, but he left a project upon which an impressive amount of work had been done. From such a bustling beginning, one would expect a rapid completion of the work, but this was not to be the case. Hindered by the state's financial reverses, the railroad was not finished until 1847. In the few years remaining before the Civil War, it had just begun to realize the hopes entertained by its creators.

The people of the 1830s, like the people of any time, could not foresee with any certainty what the ultimate result of their state's "great undertaking" would be. Nonetheless, their hopes were high as the first turbulent year of the W&A came to a close.

What would the project do for Georgia? Stephen H. Long, in a report to Governor George Gilmer in November 1837, voiced the sentiment of many in the flowery language required at the time for top-class flattery:

> The Western and Atlantic Rail Road, when viewed in its relations to the natural and artificial channels of trade and intercourse...is to be regarded as the main connecting link of a chain or system of internal improvements, more splendid and imposing than any other than has ever been devised in this or any other country. In contemplating the widely extended and incalculable benefits, in a civil or military, moral or commercial, and even in a religious point of view,

that must undoubtedly result from its consummation, we are overwhelmed with the flood of magnificent results that breaks upon us. Among these we venture to advert to one of the innumerable advantages hereafter to result from the sources above contemplated; in relation to which, the South is most deeply interested, viz, the repopulation, and reclamation of the worn out and deserted fields every where to be met with, in the older parts of all the Southern States by industrious White inhabitants, who will replenish the waste places and restore fertility to the exhausted Glebe.

With such an enterprize and the means of its accomplishment in hand, and with such prospects inviting to its vigerous prosecution, in view what destinies are too mighty, and what magnificence too exalted, for the anticipation of Georgia.

Did the Georgians of that day ever come to regret their grand, if somewhat hazy dreams for the future and the fact that they had mortgaged themselves to the hilt in the effort to make these dreams iron? Seeing what they could see, a half-finished railroad going quite literally from nowhere to not much of anywhere, did they bemoan the W&A's inception just as a major depression hit Georgia and the rest of the country? Many Georgians probably did resent what must have come to seem a luxury by the 1840s, but there were doubtless many more who shared another opinion of the large debts piled up by the state for improvements:

A great portion of this magnificent amount will be left a legacy to posterity. At the same time it becomes heir to great improvements, which will be a source to it of convenience and wealth. These improvements have helped to embarrass us, and will continue to do so for a long time. If we leave a tax on posterity, we have taxed ourselves too, and posterity will enjoy more of the benefits than we. The greatest regret is that the money borrowed has not been more economically expended — that more has not been done with the same means.

The Georgians of the early nineteenth century whose dreams turned into the W&A could return today, almost two centuries later, and trace the impact of their work on the state and particularly on the creation of the modern South's largest metropolitan area. It was, after all, the placing of the W&A's southern terminus near what is now Forsyth and Magnolia Streets, today the heart of the city, that marked the beginning of Atlanta. The importance of the W&A in not only Atlanta's birth, but also its growth, can be seen in the fact that the city is a rarity, a great metropolis that is not situated on water. Think about it. It's hard to name a major city that isn't a port of some kind. Atlanta, which was an obscure Indian-trail crossroads for centuries, started its modern life in 1838 as Terminus — which means literally end of the line.

Terminus, centered on what became known as the zero milepost, had no outstanding natural advantages. It was miles from the nearest river and nowhere near an ocean or navigable lake. It had no valuable mineral deposits to exploit. It was not on any natural route between other great cities. Its scenery, while typical of the southern Piedmont's well-treed loveliness, was not spectacular. Nature had given the area no special gifts. What the future city had was a stake in the ground and a big dream inherited from those who risked a very large roll of the dice on their conviction that Georgia must have a genuine transportation network or abandon any hope of greatness. Over the years, as branches snaked from the zero milepost to the terminus points of the state's major private railroads, their belief was rewarded. Not only Atlanta profited. For the first time, the enormous state was physically and economically connected, and in proof of the importance of the connection, the southern terminus point of the W&A became the state capital.

There were challenges along the way. Construction took longer than anyone had anticipated, and the expenditure was larger than initially envisioned. In the intermediate run, the completed line was commandeered by the North during the Civil War. In the long run, the line's maintenance did not receive the same care and attention as had its beginning. But that's another story. Ours ends with the observation that great dreams often have great costs, but it is only from such dreams that the future truly grows.

The End

Afterword

This study, which originated in a graduate class taught by Dr. Merl E. Reed at Georgia State University, is based on research at the Georgia Archives in original government documents and contemporary newspapers.

All maps were drawn especially for this study.